Next you need to find the right way to wrap up the bad things that are causing you to feel anxious and isolated. So, Knowing you don't want the Sad, Frightening Times to remain. You need to put your past problems and feelings of insanity behind you Today! That means realizing YOU NEED TO CHANGE THE OLD NEGATIVE WAY YOU FEEL ABOUT THINGS. Thinking that wrapping it up way, you need to realize that beginning insight includes Wrapping Up your anxiety, isolation, tears, fears, sad memories, and crazy times of the day that you don't want to stay! That's why, with the Future arriving as everybody is starting to Wrap up presents. Not wanting to wrap up the PRESENT Today. To make sure you Have a Happy New Year, you need to put your tears, fears, and unhappy year away. And as you Wrap up the past you left behind...in Time, you will enjoy the PRESENT in life, called a new day and a healthy mind!

Next, to turn all negative thoughts around, as you Keep getting closer to wrapping it up. To CHANGE YOUR BAD ATTITUDES, you need to Stop feeling anxious, isolated, and confused. Then, instead of living with worry, loneliness, self-abuse, and trials, you need to fill your life with joyful presents and nice times. That's why before the old year passes by you need to realize for YOU to CHANGE YOU... you must put the pain of the past behind. Then as you find the peace, and contentment in your mind that you lost along the way. To make anxiety, isolation, and fear disappear you must find a way to celebrate the New Year that is not here! So, to thrive in the New Year that is not here, don't lose your mind while WRAPPING UP THE PAST IN YOUR PRESENT. Bottom line, leave the worry and pain behind!

Likewise, to have a good day and a Happy New Year, never wrap up the BLESSED GIFT OF THE FUTURE that will be coming near! And, instead of wrapping up the good things in life... trade your anxiety and isolation in for the Gift of happiness, contentment, and nice times. Next as YOU CHANGE YOUR MIND.... let the Past go! Then, living life by looking Forward to a Happy NEW Year, and nice Today, you will find when YOU CHANGE YOUR MIND, it's easy to take your worry and isolation away. And that's good to know, because the exciting, awaiting great Tomorrow will be located in the Present of the PRESENT that has come your way! So, to be happy with who you are...DON'T LOOK FOR YOUR Present in the Past! Next to find that these things are True all you have to do... is Ask YOU to fix YOU. Then as you Believe you Can be released from anxiety; Relief will be given to you. Bottom line, when you Seek the Peace you need, you will find Release, from your anxiety and negativity. And finally, by trusting Jesus to heal you... Knock and know in Faith you can open any door! Now to realize the Best is yet to come into your life. For relaxing insight that will help you decompress read (Matthew 7:7)

2. That means as you are asking, seeking, and needing to find relief from your misery. You must start Teaching Yourself how to be mentally free from your feelings of worry, isolation, confusion, self-abuse, and anxiety. That's why, to know the reason for any season, you must realize the gifts of all the sweet, nice times will always be found in what you need to receive. Bottom line, the peace you seek, likewise the mental freedom you need to find, will be found in the PRESENT of Time. And that gift of Serenity will always be found in your heart, soul, and mind. That means, AS YOU CHANGE YOU, BY STOPPING YOUR BAD, MAD, SAD, SELF-ABUSIVE MENTAL ATTITUDES. You will find acceptance and peace wherever you go. Therefore, shore to shore, when you ask Jesus Christ to guide your life, and to help you with your therapy. For one reason, for every season, after you find what you're looking for... you will never want anything more! So, knowing by Grace and Faith you have Everything you will ever need to be healthy in your mind, and to be set free inside. That means, Jesus Christ will Forever be the best present of the PRESENT, Who will free you from your feelings of worry, isolation, and anxiety.

Therefore, shore to shore by accepting the Present of the PRESENT, and the GIFT of the FUTURE too. Knowing you need a healthy mind to get you through life. Realizing if you will just start being nicer to You that your growing pressure will begin to end. In your review, that's when you will find the Present of the PRESENT, also known as the GIFT and the Present of the FUTURE. And that gift also Present will always give you a reason to feel good about Everything! Then finding strength inside your mind, that insight will end your isolation also anxiety. And that SELF therapy will make you whole inside. Yes, that's great insight that will help you day and night, because WHEN YOU CHANGE THE WAY YOU LOOK AT TIME, by turning away from your feelings of isolation, self-imposed misery, and anxiety. You will see when you look for the Best things in life that the Present of the PRESENT also called the Gift of the Future, will bring you peace. Next To find the guidance that will free your mind, read (Luke 12:25).

3. So, realizing worrying will not add one hour to your life. Likewise realizing worrying will not solve any problems that come into your days or nights. Additionally, knowing all worrying will do is bring on floods of immobilizing anxiety. As worrying makes you feel isolated and alone. You need to know TO BE HAPPY YOU MUST STOP WORRYING about the things that have happened, or the things you fear might be coming along! And instead of worrying you need to enjoy the beginning of each day that will be leading you to the next morning! Bottom line to be content all the time, and to enjoy the Future, you need to look forward to your Present of the PRESENT that will always be leading to the Gift of a Healthy Mind. So, to be clear, and to be full of good cheer, going into the New Year, you must enjoy your PRESENTS Present by not fearing the Gift of the Future that's coming near. That means, AS YOU CHANGE THE WAY YOU FEEL ABOUT LIFE, by leaving the past behind. Becoming a new you... Happily, You will be able to live in your PRESENT, without worry, anxiety, fears, tears, isolation, or crying too.

Then realizing if you will Stop Lying to yourself about how you are feeling. While looking deep into the Dark Side of your Mind. By Facing up to how you are dealing with the resulting problems. No longer keeping Secrets bottled up inside… that means YOU CAN CHANGE YOUR LIFE! That's why, knowing You Need Help, that SOS insight is the first step to a healthy mind! Next realizing only, YOU… can find the way to help YOU! By facing your fears and anxieties that bring on feelings of isolation and misery. Knowing you are FINE and are Not Crazy. You will find when you think about THINGS the RIGHT way, YOU CAN CHANGE YOUR LIFE Today! Then that SOS Truth will end your isolation. Yes that's good news because in your present of the PRESENT, you can face up to what is bothering you. So, finding Who can HELP YOU…while being strong and courageous everyday… you can free yourself from depression. That's why when you find the way to CHANGE YOU! You will see YOU… CAN also END YOUR ANXIETY. Next to enjoy your self-help therapy read this awesome scripture that changes everything (Joshua 1:9)

4. Bottom line with you wanting to be strong of heart and courageous in your mind, You must MAKE SURE YOU CHANGE YOU... IN TIME! And to find the difference in your life between crying and smiling, no matter what is happening, you need to Quit being Confused. Likewise, You need to Stop Being Frightened and Start concentrating on the Nice Sights in your days and nights. Then in that new Life Changing Decision when you choose to smile, and not to cry.. No matter what keeps Confusing and Frightening you day and night you need to realize, happiness in life has nothing to do with what is happening on the Outside! Instead, joy and mental healing, have to do with what is happening Inside your heart, soul, and also mind. So, knowing every good and perfect Present comes from what you do, see, think, and Believe. You must realize that Peaceful wise insight will be the nice present of the new PRESENT, you need to find that will end your misery. Now, for more self-awakening read (James 1:17)

5. Next, knowing that every Perfect gift comes from what you Need. To make sure, you are not upset over earthly short supplies and high prices that will take away the happiness you seek. You also need to know the Present you buy, or gift you sell, will never free you from your feelings of isolation and anxiety. Instead, you need to make sure you are healthy in your mind. And to do that, you need to find happiness inside while you appreciate the small things happening in your days and nights. Likewise, you need to realize that Self-Healing insight has just stopped your trapped Self-imposed thoughts about confusion and apprehension. That means, WITH YOU CHANGING YOUR MIND ABOUT THINGS YOU WANT IN LIFE…Realizing the Earthly Presents you want underneath your tree, are not what you Need! KNOWING THE PRESENT, and GIFT OF THE FUTURE will be what you need to Receive! You will see, it's NOT what you Buy or Sell that makes you happy! It's the Gift of Insight… that will bring clarity, change, and peace into your mind and life. So, knowing if you don't have what you want, you have all you need. Believing… will keep You healthy! For release from anxiety (Matthew 21:22)

6.So, in review to be set free from earthly things, while thinking about The PRESENT and the gift you need to Bring to YOU, is it better to be given presents in your PRESENT? Or is it more fulfilling for you to know that the Present IS the Gift of your Future and your PRESENT too. Well, that LIFE CHANGING insight depends on if you know the Present, is the Gift of your PRESENT, also beginning of your Future Blessings. And that Insight that changed the PRESENT into a Present, has just nicely released you from feeling anxious and isolated. That means in that Present that changed Everything in the PRESENT... as your Present, became your PRESENT, if You Will Just BELIEVE that you are healthy, you will see Jesus Christ has given you the GIFT of a Peaceful mind. And Knowing that there is NOTHING Wrong with your mind, that present of the PRESENT, and provision of the FUTURE, will CHANGE YOU, and CHANGE YOUR LIFE! Likewise, realizing today will be great, that Change Of Your Mind, will Stop your growing frightening feelings of anxiety. And that's good to realize, because the gifts of the PRESENT will free your mind. For more self-insight, read these lines found in (Psalm 118:24) that will heal your life.

7.Therefore, knowing that today is the day the Lord has made. Meaning that today is the Present of the PRESENT that you need to enjoy and Not Waste. To find the best things in life, you know at Chris-mas you will receive presents and gifts from friends also family. But of note, none of these earthly adult presents, gifts, or children's toys, balls, and dolls... will Ever be coming from Santa Clause. Because after all, in that Life "Clause" there will never be such a thing as an invisible fat man in a red suit, or a mythical toy shop located below the north pole. So, receiving pre-fabricated presents and store-bought gifts, realizing Earthly fleeting things will be exchanged, dropped, swapped, destroyed, broken and will turn up missing. Knowing factory made things will leave you feeling empty and alone. Likewise realizing worldly gifts, also presents, like ties, kites, and even diamond rings will be lost, stolen, given away, or sold. That makes the disposable gifts of CHRIS-mas desolate, and disappointing.

But WAIT... there is something else you need to know if you are to start **ENJOYING ALL OF YOUR PRESENTS**. Because there is **ONE Life CHANGING** gift and Soul Saving Present you need that will end your feelings of isolation and anxiety. And that is the Daily Present and Gift you should receive... that you can Save and Keep. Happily, that Treasure will Forevermore be, the Present of your **PRESENT** and the Gift of your Future leading to your release from your isolation and anxiety. That's why to have every **PRESENT**, and **TOMORROW** you will ever need, You must **CHANGE YOUR MIND ABOUT** wanting earthly things. And instead to find what you **NEED**; you need to Receive, The Sweet Gift given to you on **CHRIST-mas Eve**. That means, to have The **FUTURE** present **PRESENT**... you must realize when you look forward to life, as you eliminate the Crazies from your days. You have been given Everything you will need to End your trapped feelings of anxiety and isolation. Now to prove to you somebody really does care, please read this beautiful, delightful scripture that will change your year. (Isaiah 9:6)

8. That's why as you go through life you need to realize the gift of the PRESENT, will Never be found in earthly things. Instead, the Present of the Future will be found in the Gift given to us on CHRIST-mas Eve. That means, you need to remember as you go through life to have a healthy mind, the way you look at TODAY matters! Likewise, the Things that you do... and say... will always be important to your Tomorrow. Therefore, shore to shore, realizing the things you say, do, also Believe can CHANGE YOUR History. Positive uplifting words will replace your anxiety with peace. Next to bless your heart in all you do and say. When you look at things the Right way. By seeing things positively, that Change will free you from your feelings of isolation, also worry. That means to receive your Present you need to put the emphasis on your healthy mind! And knowing its Jesus Christ who has given you a great life. You will know WHO is important in life! Then in that excitement, guidance, encouragement, and divine HELPFUL observation, the things CHRIST keeps doing and saying will HELP you know that you are never isolated or alone. Now to find more self-healing that you need, please read (Ephesians 4:29)

9. But WAIT.. what if you don't think what you say, Believe, or do matters! And with some of you thinking nothing nice or good will remain the same or last. As the old year has been transitioning into the present day while the future has already begun to pass. Realizing grasping the truth... that the existing PRESENT will soon be changing into the past equally fast. Right now, IF YOU HAVE NOT FOUND THE HELP YOU NEED TO RECEIVE, you are finding living in the sad, bad, anxious, and isolated yesteryear that none of these Trapped things are making you happy. And as time has been sliding by, with you fearing nothing good or nice will ever remain. With you saying Crazy things, thinking you Are Insane! You have seen, Staying on the right track has not been an easy task. That means living in your negativity while being miserable, has Not brought you happiness! But WAIT does that have to be the case? Or IF YOU CHANGE YOU...will there be a way to find Something GREAT! Well to answer that new inquiry, and to never fear the hourglass as time passes away, you must realize, only YOU can Open Up your eyes today! And, as you allow Jesus Christ to Help free you from your anxiety and doubt you will find the way to release yourself from your Mental Trap. For more self-release please read (John 14:27)

10. That's why to find the peace you need in your life, DO NOT BE TROUBLED. DO NOT DOUBT. And to stop feeling anxious and isolated STOP BEING AFRAID! Then realizing no matter what pain or worry comes into your life, that Jesus Christ will guide you to the nicer times. By following The STAR... Who the WISE MEN, AND WISE WOMEN OF TODAY still search for, and find. Happily, that's more Divine Guiding insight that will let you know you are not alone in your life! So, looking for deliverance, and enlightenment, the Wise Men and Wise Women of Today, who are always SEARCHING for things, including guidance, truth, and relief, will realize when you find what you need, you will also find the release you seek from your anxiety. Likewise realizing Jesus will always be there to pick up the pieces of your heart. You will see when life is through torturing you and ripping you apart. By Helping You free yourself from feelings of confusion, loneliness, and uncertainty, Jesus will deliver you from your growing anxiety. That means day and night as you follow the STAR of your life. You will rejoice with love and appreciation because You will be, One of the Wise Men or Wise Women who turn away from your doubts, by ending fear, while stopping trials, and finishing their isolation! Read (Matthew 2:10)

11. But WAIT, what if you are not following The STAR. What if your life is full of doubt and hardships. So, knowing the release from confusion is part of the freedom you need. How many times have you wondered who you are, where you are going, and if you really are losing your mind, also going crazy? Well knowing the answers to these life-changing questions... will help you locate the end to your anxiety and isolation. No longer needing to worry about anything. You will realize that Worrying Accomplishes Nothing!! And as you change your life by Never stressing over the things you cannot control. No longer feeling isolated or alone these directional insights will be good to know! So, finding out what's going on Inside your mind. Realizing in confusing times you Can cope with your problems. By Ending your self-abuse and Changing the doubt that comes out of your mouth! That nice released, enlightening insight will give you clarity and will end your anxiety! Then No longer living in uncertain times. You will find being Healthy in your Mind, while Telling everybody that Jesus Christ changed Everything in your life! That free insight... will end your worry, confusion and will give you guidance.

And in that guidance to stop feeling isolated and alone, you need to stop being so confused. Next To end your confusion, you need to stop being so hard on yourself. And to find the release from worry... you need to figure out who you are, also what you want to be doing. Then concentrating on Who You Need to be, knowing what you are saying will always be important to your sanity. You will find when you can stand up in front of everybody and Praise Jesus Christ glorious name for all to see. By being Your Own Therapist, realizing Jesus is Guiding You In Your Therapy! You will realize the real Present of the PRESENT, and GIFT OF THE FUTURE has everything to do with ending your isolation and anxiety. Then replacing those trapped things with freedom and serenity. Knowing WHO will Help you end your feelings of loneliness and separation... realizing its Jesus WHO will Help release you from your mental traps, and stress. THAT NORMALICY WILL CHANGE EVERYTHING IN YOUR LIFE. That's when changing the Crazy way... you think about things, while making sure Untrue and Fearful things don't come out of your mouth! You will find the Freedom from your confusion will be found in the mentally sound way you POSITIVELY deal with your Doubt! Now for more healing that changes lives read (1 Peter 5:7)

12. Then knowing how to Positively deal with stress, doubt, and anxiety while standing up to your problems also trials, many wise people will come into your life to help you get through the hard times. Next, knowing others do care for you. Realizing the release from your confusion comes from You! By Releasing your mind from negative turmoil. Those around you will guide you to the mental peace you need. In that guidance You will see friends, and family, are not the problem, bad guys, or enemies... Instead, those who care for you are there to help guard your heart, mind and also sanity. That's why, realizing there are many in your family, or others in life, who want to make sure you make it through your scary times. That insight will help you realize you are not isolated or crazy! That's why, trusting your friends and family, as everyone is trusting Jesus Christ to guide them. You will no longer feel alone. So, to deal with things positively MAKE THE CHANGE THAT CHANGES YOU! Then you will realize with Jesus being The STAR, who guides your life, and blesses your heart. Release from your Crazy Self-Made Traps will always be found in the PEACE you need to seek in the PRESENT, and in TRUTH you need to find, called Freedom From Insanity! Now be released from uncertainty read (Jermiah 33:6)

13. Next by CHANGING THE WAY YOU LOOK AT THINGS, you will be able to look forward to something good, secure, prosperous, and exciting that will soon be arriving. Then happily looking forward to what has yet to be, by leaving the past behind, you will be able to say goodbye and good riddance to unhappy things that should Not Haunt Your Mind. And as you say Goodbye to your crazy ways, and good riddance to your tragic Traps. Knowing what you are leaving behind you is History! With you realizing you no longer need to live in the past with your anxiety, isolation, and misery. Those tragic traps, and bad decisions will go away fast. Therefore, to find the peace that lasts, and that will never depart, you need to Leave your fear, sad choices, tragic Traps, and broken hearts in the past. And as, you CHANGE your darkness into light, while facing your happy future. By looking for the good things to arrive. You will find your presents PRESENT today that will last. Next as you accept the Healing that will always be waiting for you. You will know Jesus Christ will Change you, and heal your Life too! And in the same way knowing Jesus has taken Away the Crazy Darkness in your Time. That's a great wise men and wise women gift for every soul, heart, and mind. Read (Isaiah 43:18-19) for more insight.

14. But WAIT, what if you are still living in the dark! What if you are broken and lost? And if so, is there a way to get out of the dark and mend a broken heart? Is there a way to Change what needs to be fixed before you fall apart. YES there is... but first you must Forget the bad, tragic, masked, sad things in your past. Next to start over you must come out of the shadows and Fix One Worry at a Time. That means you should not try to solve all problems at once. Instead pick one part of your broken heart that needs mending... and Fix it! Next After you solve that problem... Fix another! Then with you becoming whole... your HAUNTED HEART... will not be shattered apart. Bottom line, Fixing hard times one by one, not being overwhelmed with the other broken parts, you will find when you CHANGE YOU.. you Can Get Out Of The Dark! That's why, to find the guiding light inside... you need to know, once you SEE what is right in front of your eyes, you will be able to Fix what is broken inside! Then solving your troubles, realizing they were Not awful problems at all. By healing your mind, You will Find you no longer have to feel anxious, worried, broken, lost, alone, stressed, fearful, or isolated.

Then in the change that CHANGED YOU....
AS YOU LET YOUR LIGHT SHINE THROUGH!
YOU WILL BE ABLE TO HELP OTHERS TOO!..
That means helping others change their mind.
Telling them how YOU have Changed You....
That HEALED insight will Help EVERYBODY face
their problems also trials. That's why having a
released mind that is no longer fearful of living
life. By finding the Help you need with Jesus
Guiding You In Your Therapy... you can solve ALL
problems, while ending your anxiety. Next You
will be able to bring serenity, comfort, and help
to Others as You find Peace! Bottom line, WHEN
YOU CHANGE YOU...you will be able to help
others end their feelings of worry, confusion,
isolation, and anxiety too. Then finding the way
to mend your broken heart, by realizing You can
keep You... from falling apart! Your starting over
insight will be full of solutions to all problems
that reside inside your mind. Then letting your
light shine, by giving you insight! You and others
will experience the growing Healing from Jesus
Christ. And that Guidance will make sure you,
your friends, and family find a way to never
worry, or feel broken inside. Read (Matthew
5:16) to find out how everybody can be happy.

15. Next coming out of the dark shadows, while allowing your light to shine. As you let the Change in your mind, Change your life. By receiving the peace, you need. As you Enjoy your therapy. You will finally start to mend your broken heart and end your misery. Then being a light in the dark...as Others see you Change, they will know you have started to solve your problems in the Right way! So, realizing in the Solution Of Your Confusion... that Wisdom will be found! Likewise realizing it's what happens inside your mind, that will End your Doubt and CHANGE YOUR LIFE. Knowing everybody can be Wise if they find their release inside. That's why, to be a wise man, a wise child, or a wise woman, you need to see that Jesus is the one guiding you in your Life! That means WHEN YOU COME OUT OF THE DARK... there is no problem you TWO cannot solve! So, realizing in wisdom there will be Freedom from life's pain, devastation, fear, anxiety, and heart break. Likewise realizing the Above to be true in your heart, soul, and mind too. By turning your back on your problems, failures, and disasters. You will see when you leave your Haunted History and Dark Shadows behind! The coping wisdom inside your mind, given to you by Jesus, will make you wise! This scripture will change your life. (James 1:5)

16. That's why being wise, to find the change you need to find inside; you must leave the dark Times of your mind behind. BUT WAIT.. what if you are Not wise! What if in your lack of wisdom, you are unable to see what's right in front of your eyes? Bottom line, what if staying in the Darkness of your mind, you have not found the way to solve the problems in life. That's why, searching to find what you are missing, you need to know where you can find it. Knowing why it departed and where you can seek it, will help you realize why it was important. Next to realize what's lost, also to know why it needed to be received, that bright guiding insight will let you see why you need to Celebrate when you locate it. And as you take care of it, knowing why it was important, that wise experience will help you know how to Keep it from harm, also how to safeguard it from being lost! Next, knowing what you are searching for, to never lose IT, that TRUTH will give insight into Why it was Received in the first place. That's why Seeking, Finding, Receiving, and Knowing what you need to BELIEVE will CHANGE YOUR LIFE! So as, you search for PEACE that's missing. As you find RELEASE from feelings of isolation and anxiety. You need to Stay away from the dark times, SO YOU DON'T LOSE YOUR MIND!

Then being wise realizing Change Is The Key. You will find by coming out of the Dark shadows of misery... you Won't Lose Your Mind or Sanity. That means when you MAKE THE CHANGE YOU NEED. You will find Peace, Release, and Wisdom will Change Everything. Then ending feelings of isolation and anxiety while replacing those lonely feelings with serenity and celebration. You will see when you receive The Key To The Freedom you need... your MIND will always be one of the most Important Things To FIND and KEEP! So NEVER WANTING YOU TO LOSE YOUR MIND! Knowing what you Keep searching for will always be the wisdom and Help you need to solve your fear and anxiety. You will be able to take care of your heart by safeguarding your Mind. At, the same time You will make sure your soul will never be missing, lost, or left behind! And that's divine missing, lost, located, and found WISE insight that has to do with Jesus Christ Changing Your life! That's why, realizing your Present of the PRESENT, connected to the Gift of the FUTURE should never be missing. When you let Jesus Help you end your feelings of isolation and anxiety. You will see when you ask, seek, and receive after Finding THE KEY, you will never go crazy! Now to keep you from feeling anxious and isolated in life, also to prove somebody cares all the time, read these lines in (Matthew 7:8) that will release your mind.

17. Bottom line, seeking Peace On Earth, you need to find the Peace inside your mind that you are missing. That means on your journey TO FIND THE CHANGE YOU NEED your heart, mind, and soul must find a safe place to go home so you can be free from your agony. Therefore, to stop feeling lonely you need to free yourself from your DARK thoughts about isolation, fear, and anxiety. Next you must find the sheltered place where your heart, likewise mind, will be released from your feelings of harm, self-contempt, distrust, fear, personal abuse and insanity. Bottom line, to enjoy your nice homecoming and to find Release inside your mind, you must free yourself from your Tragic Traps YOU SET to defeat your life! Next to find THE Key that guards your heart and keeps you safe from harm, you must change the way you think about things! Then finding a safe place in your mind, while no longer suffering with anxiety. The Truth is if you give them a chance everyone will Like you! Likewise, WHEN YOU CHANGE YOUR MIND about life, knowing Jesus will make sure no harm comes to you. When you befriend and trust others, you will see... because YOU... changed the negative way YOU feel about things into positive thoughts. THE Key To life will guard heart. Then as your mind gets clearer, also stronger as you go, you will be a blessing to everyone you meet also know. read (Psalm 121:7).

18. But WAIT, what if still being in harm's way, and Not changing, you don't feel the same. What if you don't trust anybody! What if you don't have any friends. What if your family is missing. What if you are isolated, and lonely. And if you cannot find THE Key, also if you cannot be happy with the things you have in life, how can you Change Time if these POOR ME TRAPS stay the same! Well, TO MAKE SURE EVERYTHING CHANGES... you have to go back to the BEGINNING that CHANGED EVERYTHING. That means, it does not matter if you are isolated or lonely, because Jesus will always be there to help get you through the hard times! So, knowing Jesus Will Always Be THE KEY To Everything...We know when we let Jesus Change Us... no matter what Crazy thoughts or Frightening events life brings our way.... we will be Okay! That means when you realize Jesus cares, then you can care for You, and others too! Next when you start caring for you, and others, by ending your feelings of inadequacies, isolation, and anxiety.. you will Change... In Time! And when you change your mind... then you, and those around you...will be able to Change life! And that Change will Change, Everything Overnight!

That's why, to get out of your mental trap's things must Change. Next to find the CHANGE THAT WILL CHANGE EVERYTHING you must find the way to be released from your anxiety. Then to find Freedom in your mind, you must realize that Change means, NO MATTER WHAT YOU HAVE, OR WHAT YOU DO.. OR WHO YOU ARE, WITH JESUS BEING YOUR SHEPHERD, KING, AND SAVIOR... JESUS CHRIST WILL CHANGE YOU! Therefore, shore to shore, we all know the LOVE AND CARING FROM ABOVE, FOUND IN SELF-HEALING THERAPY, WILL ALWAYS BE FOR EVERYONE! That means, as Jesus holds us in his Loving arms and carries us close to his heart, PEACE will always be THE KEY WE NEED to be Mentally Healthy! Bottom line, as Jesus leads those who have gone astray, while Jesus Defeats the devastation Satan brings our way. When you CHANGE, Jesus will always guard your Heart and liberate your mind from the Harmful DARK thoughts that Haunt life. That's why to be free of anxiety and to stop all feelings of isolation YOU NEED TO BELIEVE... THE KEY, will bring you relief! To find comfort read (Isaiah 40:11)

19. That means Knowing Jesus is THE Key to everything kind. Also Knowing There Is a Way to Change Your Crazy Mind. Right now, you can celebrate everything nice, big, or small happening in your life. And that's important, because if you don't appreciate the little amazing things that make up your lifeline you won't find the best things IN TIME. So, thinking about things Big and Small what does being Peaceful, and mentally free have to do with ending anxiety. Well, it means WHEN YOU FIND THE KEY and THE CHANGE YOU NEED, BY CHANGING YOU... you will Appreciate everything! Then as you enjoy the Mental Health and SELF RELEASE that comes from the Gift of Peace. No matter who you are, as long as you know Jesus, Your Savior will always be Your Help, Your Shield, Key, and Strength in times of trouble, misery, also strife. So, knowing that Jesus will Change You, that Mentally Healing Insight will bring purpose into your sunrise! Bottom line, realizing everyday Jesus Christ will give you a new, beautiful reason to Celebrate life, everything will work out alright. That means, as you depend on the Lord's Shield and Strength, while becoming less anxious, and not worried about everything in your life.. You will be getting stronger in your mind! Next as you start healing your heart. You will be able to Forgive those who Broke It Apart! Now to keep healing your mind... Please read (Psalm 28:7)

20. That's why knowing your strength comes from what's in your heart. Likewise realizing the shield that protects your mind comes from the Help you need to find before your life gets ripped apart. Realizing, finding the Peace you need in your days and nights has everything to do with you no longer Mourning the morning's light! Making that KEY statement THAT WILL CHANGE YOUR LIFE, that Free insight will also save your mind! BUT WAIT, Knowing there are still a few of you, who ARE MOURNING SOMETHING THAT HAS BEEN RUINING YOUR LIFE. In your confusion with you unable to face your grief and isolation. That means, a few of you are still Mourning your mornings. And having no way to go home, that's Not Okay! That's why, when you feel abandoned, it's time for you to SEE THINGS A DIFFERENT WAY! Therefore, shore to shore it's time for you to stop being lonely and isolated. And instead of Mourning what you left behind, it's time for you to Go Home and put your hard times behind! Therefore, to stop Mourning... you need to remember when you are Down and Broken...that is the time to Change Things! Today, is also The KEY time to Mend, then Fix Your Brain! That's why, when you Stop your feelings of confusion, isolation, Mourning, and anxiety, by finding Peace in your mind. NOW IS THE TIME, to tell others... How You Changed your life! For self-release read (Mark 5:19)

21. Therefore, as the Lord's strength and insight has Changed your mind about how you think about time! Knowing, as your BAD, TRAPPED, NEGATIVE attitudes have switched into Positive thoughts... With you being stronger in your mind than you realized. You have just released Yourself from your self-made TRAP of mental Anxiety! That's why, no longer Mourning the morning, while thinking about things POSITVELY. Feeling better about you. You are ready to Go Home! And making that nice LIFE CHANGING decision to let Others back into your life. You are now ready to show Them, you have solved your feelings of isolation, grief, anxiety, and doubt. Bottom line, leaving your Mourning behind, realizing you have CHANGED YOU, while ending your confusion. You are ready to go home for CHRIST-mas too! But WAIT... what if you don't have a home to go to! And that's a fair question, with a Happy Beginning... because having a home to go to... Depends On You! That means your home will be found wherever your heart and soul go. So, wanting to make sure you can ALWAYS Go Home. By defeating your self-imposed traps of agitation, anxiety, and isolation. Likewise CHANGING EVERYTHING IN TIME. When you Go Home and tell others how Jesus released and freed you from your feelings of Mourning, loneliness, anxiety, resentment, anger, and other trials. By healing your broken heart, and fixing your mind, also renewing life... YOU CAN ALWAYS GO HOME, ANYTIME! Now to go home read (Luke 8:39)

22. That's why, TO GO HOME ANYTIME! You need to realize; you can Also Go HOME IN YOUR MIND! That means, even if you have no home to go to, by Remembering the nice times... YOU CAN GO HOME ANYTIME! Likewise, by putting the Grieving Memories behind, you can also go back to the HOME YOU LEFT BEHIND. And that's good to know, because with everybody in the past and PRESENT... putting up trees and buying Presents. You need to realize Memories, Home, and Trees will ALWAYS be important to your sanity, because trees mark the Reflections of Time. And Home is something you always Can find! So, Realizing the tree, you put up at Home... or in your Mind... will forever mark the Memories and PRESENTS going by. You will find as time keeps fading away, To GO HOME ANYTIME, the Present of Peace... NEEDS TO BE inside your mind! Then Knowing JESUS CHRIST WILL ALWAYS BE THE Present of the PRESENT, AND THE GIVER OF HOME and MEMORIES! To make your FUTURE GREAT, AND TO ENJOY YOUR OLD also New TIMES EVERYDAY! In your Change, You will find relief from your isolation, self-abuse, and confusion, when you GO HOME. Likewise, when others see THE KEY CHANGE in you, they will know Jesus will ALWAYS be the Present of the PRESENT, and Future FAMILY TREE who brings Happiness, Peace, Home, and Sweet memories to every-Body. To find happiness read (1 John 2:17)

23. Therefore, knowing to be happy, that the Present of the PRESENT must be found and received. While realizing the things of the world will go missing. To End your seasonal feelings of isolation and anxiety, you need to realize it's not Santa Clause or Chris Kringle coming to town. That's why, to know who will always be found, and for you to know who you need to be searching for, You must know IT'S JESUS WHO WILL FOREVER BE AROUND. That means, it's Jesus Christ who will always be in found in your heart, soul, mind, and town! Next to be free and happy, you must read the CHRIST-mas Story, so there won't be any questions about why DAILY we KEEP Celebrating! Then realizing Santa Clause has nothing to do with CHRIST. Likewise knowing Santa Clause will NEVER be coming to town. But also knowing that JESUS CHRIST will always be found! With the year also THE light evaporating right in front of your eyes. As another sun goes down, you need to realize for you to stop feeling depressed and stressed, it will always be our SAVIOR Jesus, Who came to defeat worry, anxiety, also depression! That's why year after year as Jesus gives you the gifts of Peace and the PRESENT. You need to realize it will always be Jesus Christ who will CHANGE EVERYTHING... in TIME! To receive Peace read. (Luke 2:13)

24. So, realizing you are looking for Peace in your life. With you wanting to find goodwill toward the people that's been missing. Knowing all the things said in this book's Present... are True, and Right. Just like that it is CHRIST'S TIME ONCE MORE for Everybody! That means it is AGAIN the Night Before Forevermore! So, knowing CHRIST-mas will always be EVERYDAY like the day before! After reading this book that has talked straight to your soul, heart, and mind. You now know how to Not fall for the CLAUSE IN LIFE. You also know how to NOT FALL FOR THE CLAUSE IN Chris-mas, also in Time. And, learning how to end your feelings of isolation and anxiety, you likewise know where to get THE KEY, AND HELP YOU NEED! That's why, day and night it will always be nice to realize, because JESUS CHRIST was born, there will Never Be A Clause in your life, or a CLAUSE on Chris-mas morning! That means, by accepting the Present of your PRESENT, and Gift of your Future... Knowing on Our FAMILY TREE... Eternal Love rocked in the Cradle, then later on went to the Cross, so we can go Beyond! We know Forevermore started a long time ago!! For another Forevermore gift please read (Luke 2:13)

25. MERRY CHRIST-MAS EVERYBODY!! And sending out that Merry message we need to remember What CHRIST-mas will always be. That means we need to know CHRIST-mas means the most blessed wonderful time of the year... WILL DAILY be HERE! So, to enjoy each second of your Present leading to the PRESENT. By finding the Help You Need, let Jesus Do Your Daily Therapy!! Then finding the HELP AND KEY YOU MUST RECEIVE; you will ALWAYS have a MERRY PRESENT and A FUTURE THAT'S SWEET.

Bottom line EVERY DAY AND NIGHT while CELEBRATING JESUS CHRIST, and your HAPPY New Year. You will find that GIVEN HEALTHY KEY insight will change your life! So, to never feel isolated or anxious about life passing by, remember the present of the PRESENT, will always be leading to your Future blessing that started on CHRIST-mas EVE...That means, to receive the PRESENT of Peace.. that will take away all your feelings of isolation and anxiety, you need to know THE BLESSINGS OF JESUS CHRIST will DAILY, always be the life Changing Gifts of the Future you need to Receive that will keep you Mentally Healthy! And now for more Divine gifts that will keep GIVING...please read (Isaiah 9:6)

26. Yes indeed Merry CHRIST-mas Everybody!! But WAIT! Why did I say Merry CHRIST-mas TODAY? Didn't Chris-mas already go away! But Wait, AGAIN realizing CHRIST will never leave! Let me again say MERRY CHRIST-mas EVERY DAY! OH, but WAIT...WHAT IF YOU DON'T FEEL THAT WAY. What if you are feeling devastated and hollow because Chris-mas is over? What if you are stressed, since you did not get the awesome presents you wanted. Bottom line are you crying... because your diamond ring and other things are missing. Are you locked up in a dungeon of misery, while wallowing in a mess. Are you depressed because Chris-mas and fun are gone? Is life full of anxiety because CHRIS.... is done.

And with the CRAZIES, CALORIES, also BILLS coming due...Will there be any happiness for you? So, with Clause once more forgetting you! NOT getting what you wanted... IS CHRIST-mas through. And the answer is NO! BECAUSE HAPPILY, by finding the way to be Released from isolation and anxiety... you Did Get what you NEEDED! That means being FREE to be who you want to be. You don't have to stay depressed, nervous, or isolated. BECAUSE CHANGING YOUR MIND AND CRAZY FEELINGS ABOUT EVERYTHING! Realizing you are Seeing things clearly...Your DAILY PRESENT GIVEN BY JESUS CHRIST FOR THE REST OF YOUR DAYS.... IS YOU DON'T NEED ANY MORE ANXIETY OR ISOLATION THERAPY!

So, realizing because CHRIST-mas will always be Every Day! You now know there is a way to change your depressed, anxious, isolated attitudes too! And all you have to do... to find the greatest Present in life that has ever been given to you... IS to know everything in this book is TRUE! That means to end your depression, as you Changed! You now know the REAL REASON FOR CHRIST-mas will always be the ONLY REASON for Everything! Bottom line, you also know how to stop your feelings of depression, stress, worry, unhappiness, isolation, anxiety, confusion, self-abuse, nerviness, also misery.... Next celebrating CHRIST-mas DAILY, as YOU CHANGED EVERYTHING IN YOUR LIFE, that good PRESENT news Has Changed Your Mind! Next finding the HELP, PEACE, and THE KEY you need, by letting Jesus Oversee Your Therapy! By becoming your own therapist, you have ended your depressed, anxious, isolated, panicky feelings. That means you have been given the greatest present of the PRESENT you need to receive! Because as Jesus healed you and Freed your mind... YOU DON'T NEED ANYMORE ISOLATION OR ANXIETY THERAPY! Now to be Peaceful, Free and have a Fixed life read (Numbers 6:26)

27.So, knowing YOU DON'T NEED ANY MORE ISOLATION AND ANXIETY THERAPY. While thinking about things the RIGHT WAY. You also know how to answer these questions TODAY. Is CHRIST-MAS really over? If NOT, WHEN IS CHRIST-MAS, DID YOU MISS IT? And AGAIN, SAYING MERRY CHRIST-MAS TO YOU TODAY. While knowing in your heart also soul you know when Chris-mas was and is. To have CHRIST-mas EVERYDAY as you beat your holiday depression. You ALWAYS need to remember when you think about things the RIGHT way, the good things in life will stay! That means, WHEN YOU MAKE EVERY DATE, A DAY TO CELEBRATE SOMETHING... Stress and confusion will Not Beat You up Any day. Likewise, anxiety, isolation, self-abuse, abandonment, and depression will Not beat you down. In the same way unhappiness, uncertainty, or trauma will not beat you! Bottom line, by stopping ALL your regrets, and finishing your worry, while you end your stress also depression, and STOP YOUR TEARS... CHRIST-mas will ALWAYS BE HERE! And that is Divine news, because releasing yourself from Anxiety and Fear! Jesus Christ has given you the Daily gift of a Healthy Mind, and Many Mentally Happy Years.

So, knowing EVERY DAY and NIGHT have to do with JESUS CHRIST…Likewise Realizing by Celebrating Jesus Christ's Birthday All The Time, that EVERY DAY and NIGHT you can be HEALTHY IN YOUR MIND! Knowing CHRIST-mas will never be over! That means YOU DID NOT MISS ANYTHING! So, verifying it will always be CHRIST'S TIME, that Celebrating Truth will end your stress, and CHANGE your life's confusing situation. Additionally knowing it will always be CHRIST'S TIME, that Celebrating Gift will stop your daily depression, isolation, and anxiety, while ending your mental Chaos. And that's great to know, because when YOU CHANGE YOUR MIND, while no longer feeling anxious or isolated you will find by LOOKING FOR THE BEST THINGS IN LIFE that rescuing INSIGHT will be one of the best Presents of the PRESENT. So, knowing it always needs to be CHRIST'S TIME in your heart, soul, and mind. Remember all the time… to Give Thanks to the Lord for He is good, because Jesus Christ's LOVE, GIFTS, AND HELP, will endure forever! That means, because CHRIST-mas will always be EVERY DATE of your life. NOT NEEDING ANYMORE ISOLATION OR ANXIETY THERAPY. Your Mental Release… will be, the Happy Celebrating Gift that Keeps Giving! Now to celebrate your healthy mind read (Psalm 107:1)

28. So, Giving Thanks while knowing Jesus will always be the ONLY reason for ANY season. Seeing that Jesus will give you The Help you need to succeed and to be mentally healthy. Reading this SELF HELP book you have realized by letting Yourself Be Your Own Therapist... Jesus Christ has been in Charge of Your Therapy! That means crossing the finish line, you have found the mental health you seek. You have also realized you can be strong in your mind! That means you don't Ever have to be weak! And as time keeps passing by even with life Wrapping Up... you know EVERYTHING will be alright! Yes that's great insight, because realizing you left the bad, sad, crazy past behind! No longer being messed up in your mind. By making Time your friend! You can Celebrate Life EVERY Day and Night! Next to keep you, from Wrapping up time. As the old year begins to end, and the new year PRESENT prepares to begin again. Crossing the finish line, to find the best things in life, knowing that you have been released from your feelings of isolation and anxiety, you don't have to be afraid of the frightening Hourglass of Time! And instead of living in Fear... of what might be coming Near... making Time your Friend, by being Normal and Happy... you will be able to Celebrate the good Times, that ARE Here!

That means, you have realized you need to be Thankful, for the old year you are leaving behind, also the NEW YEAR you have yet to find! And in that life lesson, You have likewise learned, since you are ALIVE, there is a reason for you to OPEN YOUR EYES! That's why, as the New Year arrives...you have realized no matter what life does that makes you cry. By trusting Jesus Christ to make everything right you Never have to feel anxious, scared, or isolated again. Bottom line having CHRIST-mas and a HAPPY NEW YEAR every day and night! While looking for the best times in life that have yet to arrive. You have realized by learning to cope with the things that hurt also confuse you, you can find hope and happiness... In Time. So, seeing joy in the small things... you know Home, Memories, PRESENTS, and Trees can fill you with peace. Bottom line you have learned Jesus Christ has plans for you, to have a healthy mind. And as Jesus shows you the way to make your dreams, goals, and plans succeed. That means now and in the coming year... to defeat your Fear and end the Tears, by not giving into feelings of isolation and anxiety. You have realized by CHANGING YOU... YOUR LIFE, TIME, and MIND HAVE CHANGED TOO!.... Now to STOP your ISOLATION THERAPY .... read (Psalm 20:4) to end your Anxiety.

29. But WAIT, WHAT IF YOU STILL NEED THERAPY! What if you are STILL feeling anxious and isolated! WHAT IF YOU ARE STILL LIVING ON THE DARK SIDE OF YOUR PARALYZED MIND. WHAT IF YOU HAVE NOT CHANGED YOUR LIFE! So, Knowing if you are going to have a HAPPY NEW YEAR… there are some FRIGHTENING DEEP, HIDDEN SECRETS that YOU NEED TO FACE ALSO REVEAL. TO GET YOUR CRAZY MIND TO COME OUT OF HIDING… THOSE OF YOU WHO ARE STILL CONFUSED, need to Stop pretending that things are Okay and CHANGE THEM! THEN CHANGING YOUR WAYS, YOU NEED TO CHANGE YOU!

But WAIT … what if you are STILL not aware that things need to change. OR, what if you think it's too late to change. OR, What if you are terrified that change will MESS up your life and brain. OR what if you are AFRAID YOU CAN'T CHANGE. And Pretending things DO NOT need to change, wanting things to be the same way… WHAT IF YOU ARE NOT SURE YOU WANT TO CHANGE. BOTTOM LINE, WHAT IF YOU ARE AFRAID YOU CAN'T CHANGE YOUR MIND! OR… WHAT IF YOU ARE AFRAID… OF CHANGE!!!

Well, making those WHAT IF and OR inquiries, WITH YOU FLUNKING THERAPY! LET'S PRETEND things are OKAY. Let's pretend you Don't Need to Fix Anything Today. And in that goal let's also Pretend you never have to change! Bottom line lets pretend you are NOT ANXIOUS, ISOLATED, OR GOING CRAZY.

Yes let's pretend nothing needs to CHANGE IN YOUR LIFE. BUT WAIT... YOU ALSO NEED TO KNOW IT'S THAT KIND OF UNWISE THINKING THAT'S MESSING UP YOUR MIND! That means, IT'S THAT KIND OF NEGATIVE, CRAZY, CONFUSED THINKING THAT NEEDS TO CHANGE! So, knowing HIDING WILL NOT FIX THE PROBLEMS IN LIFE. Also knowing you cannot keep pretending things are fine when they ARE NOT RIGHT! Likewise realizing if you are to ever be happy... YOU MUST CHANGE YOUR MIND! To celebrate the Change that needs to arrive... You need TO STOP PRETENDING THINGS ARE FIND AND ALRIGHT!

That's why, REALIZING YOU CAN NOT CHANGE TIME, but YOU CAN CHANGE YOUR MIND and LIFE! You need to agree CHANGE, GUIDANCE, and INSIGHT will always be some of the Lords greatest FREE KEY GIFTS that will HELP show You HOW TO SURVIVE Satan's HARD TIMES! Change will also tell you what you need to know! And Guidance then Insight will get you where you need to go! So, NEEDING TO CHANGE! When you feel anxious and isolated, let JESUS CHANGE YOU!! Then in Heaven's Faithfulness as Jesus makes things better and NEW. Realizing CHANGE IS A GOOD THING for you. By changing anxiety, confusion, also isolation... into rejuvenation, transformation, then into Celebration. Realizing that every DATE there is a way to be Healthy, everything will be OKAY! And that's great Faithful news, because BELIEVING you can CHANGE... Jesus will Change YOU, Every Day! (Lamentations 3:21-23)

30. That means, before you can Wipe The Slate Clean, YOU NEED TO CHANGE EVERYTHING! Therefore, as the year is finishing You need to BELIEVE what you Learned, READ, and Heard... will give you Peace and Healing! So, giving you the Therapy KEY YOU NEED! Self-Healing will always be the guiding insight into fixing your life! That's why, as you turn your smart thoughts to what will be! As Time keeps flying by, you need to know Why that Change has arrived! Bottom line, WHAT HAVE YOU LEARNED THAT CHANGED YOUR LIFE TODAY? And as time Learns, from what it has READ! Are you aware what you Heard, has everything to do with you finding the KEY AND CHANGE you need! So, watching the year fade. What have you Learned, about ENDING anxiety, and isolation! What have you READ, that HELPED you STOP your WORRY and MISERY! And as these Healing words released your mind from the Frightening times you keep Hidden inside. Realizing, HEARD insights have to do with what is waiting for you to Find. What have you READ, HEARD and LEARNED that HAS CHANGED YOUR MIND! Bottom line, IN THE CHANGE YOU NEED to FIND, SEE, and BELIEVE... WHO will always be in charge of your Life, Time, Therapy, Peace, and Healing! One more time... WHO IS THE KEY to your Relief and Recovery!

So, wanting you to WIPE THE SLATE CLEAN. YOU NOW KNOW THE KEY TO EVERYTHING IS JESUS. And as Jesus has been Helping you see things clearly, while guiding you through your therapy! With you finding THE KEY to end your anxiety. Reading this book... I pray you have read EVERY Scripture EACH day. Next to really know what is being said, and to be successful in your Therapy, I hope you will take what you have Learned from your past regrets and make those corrections from what you have Heard and Read. Next to end your isolation as you tidy-time-up.... I pray you put the dirty things, like fears, lies, and tears behind you, while keeping them in the unhappy past! Then realizing the sad, tragic, Crazy past does not have to last! I Hope and Pray to have a HAPPY NEW YEAR... you take the Last words Said, also First words Heard and START A NEW LIFE TODAY! Bottom line, to Wipe The Slate clean, and to have a HAPPY NEW YEAR... THAT LASTS...I hope you get rid of your jealousy, trials, rage, lies, bitterness, confusion, isolation, anxiety, fear, regrets, worry, stress, depression, frustrations, and discouragements. Then as you END your mentally unhealthy Crazy ways. To find the best that arrives today. I pray that you put your NEGATIVE, DEFEATIST, DAMAGING POOR ME feelings away! Now to Stop your ISOLATION AND ANXIETY therapy, read (Ephesians 4:31) that will Change you in EVERYWAY.

31. So, wanting all bitterness, fears, and anger to be put away. While realizing the first words Said, Learned, and Heard have to do with the words' survival, hope, renewal, love, change, HAPPY, NEW, and YEAR. As the old year fades away, and the New Year arrives. To make the best of Time, you must realize what you have Learned, Read, and Heard, will end your anxiety and isolation! And as, you likewise realize at the stroke of EVERY midnight... Jesus Christ has given you yet another HAPPY NEW DAY in your life! That's when you too will see... by BEING YOUR THERAPIST, JESUS WILL ALWAYS BE IN CHARGE OF YOUR THERAPY! That means, knowing JESUS CHRIST WILL ALWAYS BE LISTENING AND HELPING you, CHANGE YOU! These sharing KEY Truths PROVE JESUS CARES FOR AND LOVES YOU! So, in review, as the Old becomes New...to never be Trapped, Stressed, Self-abused, Confused, Worried, or Afraid, you must live your life knowing Your bad, sad, Crazy, tragic ways have already ended! Then finding release from your Anxiety, Fears, and Isolation you will be able to have a HAPPY NEW YEAR EVERY DAY! Now to continue with your Celebration while finding the lifetime help you need, read (2nd Corinthians 5:17) (Matthew 24:31) (Jeremiah 29:11) (Romans 8:28) (Isaiah 41:10) and (John 3:16)

And as these scriptures, plus the others HAVE CHANGED YOU. KNOWING YOU HAVE BEEN RELEASED FROM YOUR MENTAL TRAPS. YOU WILL NO LONGER NEED THERAPY FOR ISOLATION or ANXIETY..

Saying that CONGRATULATIONS... YOUR ANXIETY AND ISOLATION THERAPY IS THROUGH! That means after reading this LIFE CHANGING book you have realized to HEAL YOUR MIND.. YOU NEED TO FIND THE KEY THAT CHANGES YOU!!! And as you CHANGED your CRAZY Poor Me attitude. You have found to be happy you must Not let your heart be troubled. Likewise, as your past fades away you have learned how to put your anxiety behind you TODAY! And to Not be frightened about what will be coming tomorrow, you have learned you need to CHANGE your mind so you can deal with the hard times in life! Additionally in Special Free therapy... you learned to Never be afraid of your Present, or traumatized by your Past, or fearful of your Future. Bottom line you have learned to Never be Afraid of Time passing by! Yes, that's HELPFUL insight, because reading this book, guided by these personally researched scriptures that highlight each message. You have found when you trust Jesus Christ, by NOT FEARING ANYTHING in your LIFE, the best in your Happy, MENTALLY HEALTHY Future will arrive!

BUT WAIT!!! WHAT IF you, or YOUR FRIENDS, AND FAMILY STILL NEED DIFFERENT KINDS OF THERAPY.

What if you, or those you know, are also dealing with OTHER troubling issues like agony, grief, stress, depression, fear, devastation, anger, abandonment, and other Trapped upsetting things that are all ruining Everything. WHAT IF after learning how to deal with Anxiety and feelings of Isolation... YOU too STILL NEED OTHER KINDS OF HELP, and Guidance! Well, that's alright, because in that Comforting clue, there are more Joslin Fitzgerald SELF HEALING books that will Show you.. how You.. can Change You! So, to find the other books, go into the stores ask, or search any distributor for Joslin Fitzgerald..

Of note you just purchased the Christmas Edition in the AND NOBODY CARES SERIES. But like the rest of the books that have their own months, and that each deal with different mental issues. You can read this book and be comforted in any season! That means like CHRIST-mas is every day. DAY ONE will always be ANY DAY OR NIGHT OF THE YEAR, anybody needs Help, Therapy, Peace, or Clarity.

Now as we come to the end of things, knowing
that will always be the beginning of Everything!
Realizing year after year that Jesus does care!
Likewise knowing being Mentally Healthy
is the Self Help needed therapy that you
just received. After fixing your mind, read
NUMBERS 6:24-26 one more time... Then you
can keep celebrating.... The nice Fact that
you, and Jesus Christ just changed your life!

Information sheet

So, knowing Daily we will all be Celebrating SOMETHING in some-way. Realizing every hour will be something to CELEBRATE. TO FIND THE WAY TO BE HAPPY ALL OF YOUR LIFE. Let's take this time to appreciate the continuing gifts and blessings we have been given. And as, we look forward to the Present of the Todays Present, lets CELEBRATE the Happy Future coming our way.

NOW, TO READ THE POPULAR BLOG CALLED AWAY BACK HOME AND FOLLOW JOSLIN FITZGERALD'S WRITING, TO READ ALONG, PLEASE GO TO JOSLINFITZGERALD.COM

to find out about Joslin Fitzgerald's 18 bestselling children's books, 5 animated movies, Hollywood projects, and the exciting coming soon 15 adventure packed novels plus PLUS to enjoy THE new A DAILY BREAK series please visit her blog and web sites at JOSLINFUN.COM, or ARISINGWRITERS3.BLOGSPOT. COM or ARISINGWRITERS.COM

Published by Circles Legacy Publishing LLC
Book design copyright © 2024
Project Manager and Team Coordinator: Mary Cindell Lynn Pilapil
Cover Design: Jim Villaflores
Layout Coordinator: Joseph Apuhin

Published in the United States of America

ISBN: xxx-x-xxxx-xxxx-x

Adult Inspirational Journal
November 15, 2024